Media Caricature of African Coolness

How to Talk About African and Look Cool

Kirby A. Manager

Media Caricature of African Coolness

KAM Media Services

P.O. Box 90321

Raleigh NC, 27675

ISBN 978-0-9839304-2-6

Printed and bound in the United States of America

Media Caricature of African Coolness

To my Mom, for all the obvious reasons

Also By Kirby A. Manager

★ *Stereotypes and Labels: The Price We Pay For The Tags*

Table of Contents

INTRODUCTION

In this book, I make a sarcastic presentation of the stereotypical image the Western media has painted of Africa. It's supposed to be both entertaining and reflective to readers from both sides of the paradigm.

On a serious note, I warn that, while some of these caricatures may be based on reality at the time, without balance and circumspection, we risk hardening the public's consciousness and causing people to become immutable, even after the media sketches have changed.

AFRICAN COOLNESS

Whether you're an academic, a politician, a researcher, an entertainer, or a student who lands the opportunity to talk about Africa, to make a good impression, there're rules to playing the game.

The traditional approach is to handle it the way you'd handle a discussion on France or United Kingdom. To be regarded as an expert today, you present facts and figures, names of cities, and personalities because any seasoned journalist won't let you walk away with mere generalizations.

The contrary, however, works perfectly when it comes to discussing Africa. To do well on the topic of Africa, select broad themes with no specifics, remove all facts and figures, and choose exotic words and phrases. This has become the Western media caricature of Africa. It plays well into some portions of the public.

In a recent national debate on CNN, a Minnesota Congresswoman, Michelle Bachman, referring to President Obama's announcement that he will be sending a hundred American troops to Uganda to help battle rebels from the Lord's Resistance Army, said, "Now with the president, he put us in Libya. He is now putting us in Africa. We already were stretched too thin, and he put our special operations forces in Africa." I'll skip clumsy geography in the remark, but comment that such generalizations work pretty well in significant parts of the Western media. To be regarded as *cool*, this should be your yardstick.

I appreciate that a significant portion of the public isn't sold on the media portrayal of Africa. Some of them have even, perhaps, had enough of the TV caricature.

Who wants to be Cool?

★ Imagine a just-arrived African immigrant who has been invited to a friend's graduation cookout party in the United States. He's new to USA. He doesn't drive. In fact, he doesn't even have a driver's license yet. He needs to make friends quickly and he needs to be seen as *cool*.

★ Or take him to be a graduate student who, miraculously, lands a television interview to talk about Africa. He sees this as once-in-a-lifetime opportunity.

★ A college professor who gets a call from a local radio or television station for an expert opinion for a news item on Africa. What an opportunity!

★ A just-returned vacationer from Africa who just needs to show how much he learned about the 'dark continent' in a mere ten days.

★ A media intern who miraculously witnessed a successful transition of power from one administration to another in Africa.

Any of these folks could represent one of the many people who tell their African story one way or the other. The African caricature we have now is the result of the composite stories told by all those folks who needed to tell their African story for one reason or the other.

Royal Introduction Doesn't Hurt

If you're the African immigrant who wants to be seen as *cool*, to make the first good impression, attempt to introduce yourself as a royal, even if the connection to an African Royal family is remote. It doesn't hurt at all. Why miss that opportunity?

Must Haves in Your Vocabulary

This is essential for all *wannabe cools*. To talk about Africa and be seen as *cool*, you can't afford to be ignorant of certain words or not be a master of them. For your hosts to enjoy your company, as a general rule of thumb, your answers to most questions should be articulated to include words such as: *genocide, corruption, poverty, ignorance, scarcity, slaughter fields, refugees, refugee camps, child soldiers, militia-molested girls.* Also very important are words like: *junta, rebel, gang, revolution, regime forces, and tribal head.* These are words you'll need to describe the African government and ministries. There will be more on this later. Unsurprisingly, you can't talk about Africa and be seen as *cool* if you're too shy or too conservative to describe abused mothers standing bare-chested by roadsides, and unrestrained prostitutes that have taken over the cities and will do anything even for nothing.

The African Child

Your description of the African child is a vital test of your understanding of the continent and your *sense of coolness*. Don't bother about the specifics—whether she's found at the refugee camp or located in the Governor's mansion. It's the description of the African child that matters. It should be as graphic as imaginable. If you've been to the bookstore or seen one of those television appeals for charitable donations for Africa, you should know the usual depiction of the African child. She's anemic, malnourished, has a protruding belly and an unequal distribution of hair on the scalp. Don't make the mistake of telling her age from her appearance. In most cases, she has a bubble of tears dripping down her cheeks. In other situations, in spite of these handicaps, she looks happy and always carries a broad, infectious smile.

The African Government

With regard to discussions about the type of government that exists in Africa, do not spend time classifying countries into: democracy, military rule, and others. If you really want to be *cool*, lump it all together and say that the Africa government is a dictatorship and everybody connected to the African government is corrupt. Any other response will draw too much confrontation and that won't be suitable for a *wannabe cool*.

To show that you're not only *cool* but perhaps even an *expert* on African foreign policy, don't use the noun *Government* often when talking about Africa. When referring to the ruling administration, opt for the word *Regime*, which is more exotic. As for the Opposition Party, my word of advice is: never use the word Opposition. It's too Western. Preferred words that are striking when referring to the Opposition party in Africa include: *The Movement, The Junta, The Resistance, The Rebellion, The Rebels,* and *The Faction.* Acceptable others are: *The Insurrection, The Sect, The Revolt, The Uprising,* and *The Splinter Group.* These are words that work on all occasions when talking about Africa in the Western media. The words *Government* and *Opposition* don't connect.

Judiciously throw in sentences such as: "During my recent trip to Africa…" or: "In a recent conversation with an African tribal head……" if you want to command respect and be held in high esteem. It's not required, but at this point, you could tap your foot and shake your head in deep nostalgia of the spiritual song the *Tribal Chief* sang as he wished you adieu.

That's so Beautiful!

The questions around beauty and the perception of beauty in Africa would be the same question many Africans in the West have answered over several decades. As someone who wants to be seen as *cool*, simply talk about how much Africans love to be fat because the fatter you are, the more beautiful you are in the African's eyes. This is the most believable version of the story so far. Why go for something else unless you have the time to defend your thesis?

It's Hot in here!

To be a *Cool* African Guy or an expert on Africa, you should absolutely be prepared to talk about the weather in African. At the least, you should be ready to answer the question, "How hot is Africa"? Simply say the coldest temperature in Africa is hotter than the warmest summer month in Miami, FL. While your hosts open their ears and eyes for more, add: "And, yet, there are no air conditioners or ceiling fans." At this point, you may get a pat on the shoulder as a sign or approval or, perhaps, a call to spend more time on that topic. As you talk about the temperature, note that your hosts may not care whether you're from Cape Town in South Africa or Ouagadougou in Burkina Faso. Don't take any pains to be specific. That's what makes it fun and will make you *cool*. Just talk about Africa.

It's Soccer or no Sports

The chitchat around sports may revolve around football and soccer and the nuances behind the names. To really make the interaction fun and be seen as even more *cool*, emphasize that the only sport in Africa is football. (Remember to give a footnote that you're talking about soccer!) If your hosts ask about hockey and cricket, tell them that, in Africa, these sports can be found only in very rich neighborhoods and these are games reserved for sons and daughters of millionaires and politicians.

.

Your Name Means….

If your name is Joseph, you may skip this. But, if you carry a 'typical' African name, expect some discussion around it. Whatever the question, just remember to make it seem luscious and be seen as *cool*. Remember that, if you do it well, you are likely to be invited again. Share the fact that every African name has a meaning and explain what your own name means and why your parents gave you that name. Don't worry about accuracy. Just find something to say. Be creative. And please say your name the way it is said in Konongo in

Ghana. Don't Americanize it. The heavier it is, the more attentive your listeners will be. And that doesn't hurt, does it? Remember, you are going for *cool!*

Be patient. It takes a while for people to learn how to say African names.

Not a Ghanaian? You may skip this. Imagine you're a Ghanaian and you happen to be called Kofi. Great! Please be prepared to answer the question regarding your relationship with Kofi Annan, the former United Nations Secretary General. To save you from spending too much time on this question and to give you a break to get something to drink, simply say yes, you and Kofi Annan are related and that

Mr. Annan is your uncle's cousin's brother's nephew. Who wouldn't believe that? If you don't mind spending too much talking about names, then go ahead and explain that Kofi Annan is called Kofi because he was born on Friday. Then, don't be irritated if the next statement is, "Then there should be millions of people with the same first name Kofi."

Before I Forget about Safaris

Who seriously wants to learn about Africa and forgets to inquire about safaris? You will be asked about safaris. Some people get irritated when asked about animals in Africa and related questions. Keep *cool* if you really want to be seen as *cool*. The question may center around whether you've been on a safari, and what you saw, and stuff like that. Answer it in a way that makes you appear *cool*. If you just returned from a vacation in Africa, why not describe the unforgettable experience of merely peeping through your hotel windows to see some of the exciting animals in Africa. Describe lions and kangaroos that invade the school football field near your hotel and, on most days, how difficult it was to get them to leave the field so kids could play games. End with how much you miss this particular experience under that blue, African sky and how you can't wait to get back to Africa. Get a little emotional even if you have to fake it!

Your Story Touches Me

To you, the immigrant, assuming you've been graphic in your description of the situation on the continent and that you have validated every sketch, then you should be prepared to answer a question such as: "So, how did you manage to come here?" If they forget to ask, bring it up yourself. Stress how everybody in Africa is struggling to move to America and describe in vivid detail the long line of visa applicants at the American embassy in Africa. Emphasize that you believe your coming to America happened by God's grace. Tell your audience that your family is exceptionally poor and you believe that God brought you to America as your last chance, and, of course, your family's last hope.

If you're in the U.S. for studies, solidify the perception your hosts have that you have no intention of returning to Africa any time soon—if ever. If somebody asks, "So do you plan to go back to Africa after school?" respond with emphasis, "Obviously no! If you had any idea what I've gone through to get here, you wouldn't have to ask that question!"

On a family level, the question will be something like, "How many siblings do you have?" You could offer a straight answer and walk away. But, you'd miss the opportunity to appear *cool*.

Note that polygamy in Africa is the norm, not the exception, in the Western media. If you can sense that presumption from the host, pause for about thirty seconds—as if you're trying to count all your siblings. Then, say something like, "I think we're six. No! We're nine. I forgot to add my three brothers from my father's side."

Walk is Nothing in Africa

Hope that your hosts will trick you into saying something about the transportation system of Africa. Even if they don't, find a way to slip it into the conversation. It will boost your credibility. Remember that discussions around the topic connect very well. It's a must to say that only millionaires or government officials have their own cars. Almost everybody else just walks, while the few privileged use the public bus. It's crucial to emphasize how an African can walk up to ten miles as if it were nothing. Say this with an innocent smile.

Leave by Playing the Devil's Advocate

Leave a lasting impression by sympathizing with the African people. If you have just returned from a visit to Africa, emphasize how your impression of the African people changed as a result of your recent visit. Describe how good, kind-hearted, hardworking, conservative, and family-oriented the African people are and how frustrated you get when the media lump the people of Africa together, as though they are just one homogeneous group of people. While doing this, never use the nouns: *Ghana, Senegal, or Zambia.* Just talk about the African people in general.

Keep in mind that airtime is money in the Western economy. So, when someone offers you the opportunity to talk about Africa, consider it a privilege. It's not every subject that makes the cut!

Stuff that won't Impress Anyone

On the other hand, if you don't care if your hosts don't think you're really *cool*, then you can risk talking about things such as:

1. Africa is a continent of fifty-four independent countries with nearly one billion people. (This is about three times the population of the U.S!)

2. The size of the African continent (30,3 million km^2) is larger than the combination of: China (9,6 million km^2), the U.S. (9,4 million km^2), Western Europe (4,9 million km^2), India

(3,2 million km²), and Argentina (2,8 million km).

3. Africa's population consists of blacks, Arabs, whites, and Indians.

4. Africans abroad remit back home about $40 billion annually and still manage to pay their mortgages and credit card balances.

5. English, French, Arabic, and Portuguese are used as the languages of instruction right from kindergarten in most African countries.

6. Like Brazil, Peru, and Australia, the Democratic Republic of Congo has one of the richest ecosystems in the world. (Have you ever heard something good about the DRC?)

7. Africa isn't a parasite on Western economy. On the contrary, Africa makes significant contributions to the global economy, with an estimated combined purchasing power of more than $2.5 trillion [source: United Nations Development Program (UNDP)].

8. The country with the world's most sustained and strongest economic growth over the last four decades is in Africa. It's Botswana.

9. According to International Monetary Fund (IMF) assessment, over the next decade, the African continent will have as many as seven of the ten fastest-growing economies in the world.

If you really want to make the situation worse, why not throw in stuff like:

1. The McKinsey report estimates that, by 2030, the continent of Africa's top eighteen cities will have a combined spending power of $1.3 trillion.

2. Africa has the only street in the world to house two Nobel Peace prize winners. It's Vilakazi Street, Soweto, South Africa. Both Nelson Mandela and Archbishop Desmond Tutu have houses on the street. (Is that significant?)

3. Africa isn't all slums. From Johannesburg to Dakar, Dares Salaam to Nairobi, Accra to Cairo, many African cities

boast   towering   skyscrapers,   complex
infrastructures,   modern   universities   and   a
sizzling nightlife that will amaze any first-time,
uninformed tourist.

4. The continent is home to some of the
most talented athletes on the planet. Every
major club in Europe includes a couple of
African athletes. Most European stadiums are
empty. (Permit a little exaggeration!) for the
four weeks African athletes leave for the
African Cup of Nations.

But let me warn you, as I have done earlier,
it's very risky to take the latter route. You may
be a big disappointment to your hosts. Any

future invitation is unlikely and above all, you will lose the most covet label: *cool.*

It was Meant to be a Joke but…

By the way, whether you ask or answer these questions, don't take my analysis personally. In psychology, it's said that humans are more likely to recall intense memories. Perhaps this is the reason it appears that our society thrives on bad news, and good news never manages to hold on to the airwaves.

I do believe there's the need for some kind of balance in the way the Western media portrays Africa. While some of these caricatures may be based on reality at the time, when they're overly played, we stand the danger of solidifying the public's perception. In time, these perceptions will become unchallengeable, even after the media sketches that gave rise to them have changed.

Consider the Western media cartoon of Africa, the sketch of the Latino with an accent, the media skit of an Arab immigrant after the September 2001 attack in the U.S. Sometimes, I wonder whether the media is carrying out the biases and concerns of the public or whether the public is being fed an overly stereotyped image of the groups mentioned. Gallup may have the data to help us answer that.

It's unfair to blame a single source for these sketches—even if that source is the media! The truth of the matter is: many African intellectuals in the West have played, and continue to play, significant roles in creating this mindset in the quest to be *cool*.

I applaud what charitable and non-governmental organizations do to improve the lives of many communities across the African continent. Unfortunately, many of these organizations create a one-sided story of the one billion people who call Africa their homeland. The danger in such one-sided stories can be huge. In fact, the consequence can be perilous as recounted by the Nigerian novelist, Chimamanda Adichie, in her speech, *"The Danger of a Single Story"*.

Acknowledgements

Most of all, I am grateful to my family for their support and patience as I maneuver to steal some time to write.

I'm also grateful to my editor Ms. Gail Lennon, who read the final manuscript and gave me confidence that I had something valuable to contribute and the green light to publish this book.

About the Author

Kirby A. Manager, PhD. is originally from Ghana but has lived in the United States for the past several years. He earned his Ph. D. in chemistry at the University of Florida, Gainesville. He's a full-time scientist in Pharmaceutical Research & Development. In his spare time, he enjoys reading and writing about issues affecting the developing world and playing soccer with his two boys. He's the author of: *Stereotypes and Labels: The Price We Pay for the Tags*. He lives in Raleigh, NC.